LOW-OXALATE RESET

Transform Your Health in 30 Days with Nourishing Recipes, Vibrant Meal Plans, and Expert Guidance

BY THE OXALATE HEROES

ALSO IN THE FOOD HEROES SERIES

Low-Oxalate Food List: The World's Most Comprehensive Low-Oxalate Ingredient List - Take It Wherever You Go!

Find Your Food Triggers: Investigate Every Food With Detailed A-Z Guide - Go Low Lectin, Low Histamine, Low Oxalate, Low Salicylate, Follow the DASH Diet, Diverticulitis Diet and More

LEGAL AND DISCLAIMER

The information contained in this book is not designed to replace or take the place of any form of medicine or professional medical advice. The information in this book has been provided for educational and entertainment purposes only.

You need to consult a professional medical practitioner in order to ensure you are both healthy enough and able to make use of this information. Always consult your professional medical practitioner before undertaking any new dietary regime, and particularly after reading this book.

The information contained in this book has been compiled from sources deemed reliable, and it is accurate to the best of the Author's knowledge; however, the Author cannot guarantee its accuracy and validity and cannot be held liable for any errors or omissions.

You must consult your doctor or get professional medical advice before using any suggested information in this book.

Upon using the information contained in this book, you agree to hold harmless the Author, and Publisher, from and against any damages, costs, and expenses, including any legal fees potentially resulting from the application of any of the information provided by this guide. This disclaimer applies to any damages or injury caused by the use and application, whether directly or indirectly, of any advice or information presented, whether for breach of contract, tort, negligence, personal injury, criminal intent, or under any other cause of action. You agree to accept all risks of using the information presented inside this book.

CONTENTS

PART ONE

THE LOW-OXALATE LIFESTYLE: UNDERSTANDING THE BASICS

1. INTRODUCTION

Welcome to *Low-Oxalate Reset*, your guide to embracing a healthier lifestyle. Our comprehensive program is designed to help you improve your overall health and wellbeing through low-oxalate eating. It may seem challenging right now - we get that - and it's our job to make it as straightforward as possible.

We put this together because, like you, we've dealt with food intolerances and oxalate issues. There's a ton of conflicting info out there, and it can be super frustrating. You might know us from our bestselling Oxalate guide (*Low-Oxalate Food List*), and the *Low-Oxalate Reset* takes it to the next level.

Before we go any further, we take our sources, references and science seriously. Oxalate Heroes guides use the respected sources listed below. We have once again used the same respected sources for our 30-Day Reset as we did for our other title. But as previously, we have to remind you to approach all food with caution when it comes to oxalates. One of the main reasons we are passionate about providing you this *program* is that the top sources disagree so often about oxalate content. Nothing in this book should be construed as medical advice. You should consult your doctor or get professional medical advice before following a low-oxalate program.

- The University of Chicago - How To Eat A Low Oxalate Diet https://kidneystones.uchicago.edu/how-to-eat-a-low-oxalate-diet/
- Harvard T.H. Chan School of Public Health https://regepi.bwh.harvard.edu/health/Oxalate/files
- Harvard T.H. Chan School of Public Health Food List https://regepi.bwh.harvard.edu/health/Oxalate/files/Oxalate%20Content%20of%20Foods.xls
- National Library of Medicine - Oxalate content of food: a tangled web https://pubmed.ncbi.nlm.nih.gov/25168533/
- University of Virginia - Digestive Health Center https://med.virginia.edu/ginutrition/wp-content/uploads/sites/199/2014/04/Oxalate-Foods-02.17.pdf
- Pitchaporn Wanyo, Kannika Huaisan & Tossaporn Chamsai - Oxalate contents of Thai rice paddy herbs (L. aromatica and L. geoffrayi) are affected by drying method and changes after cooking https://link.springer.com/article/10.1007/s42452-020-2703-6
- Urinary Stones Info - The Oxalate Content Of Food https://www.urinarystones.info/resources/Docs/Oxalate-content-of-food-2008.pdf
- Sally K. Norton Which Spices Are High In Oxalate https://sallyknorton.com/which-spices-are-high-in-oxalate/

- Low Oxalate Info Website http://lowoxalateinfo.com/
- Winchester Hospital Low-Oxalate Diet Health Library https://www.winchesterhospital.org/health-library/article?id=196214
- Low-Oxalate Diet - Mark O'Brien MD (adapted from University of Pittsburgh Medical Center https://www.markobrienmd.com/OxalateDiet.pdf
- University of Michigan Health - Foods High in Oxalate https://www.uofmhealth.org/health-library/aa166321

We urge you to go carefully and try ingredients slowly. You have 30 days (and beyond) to get this right. Everybody is different and one of the reasons people love our bestselling ingredients guide is that we continually make the point - it is not definitive and we understand how oxalate content is so hard to pin down.

Okay, now on to the good news. Once you start following the program, you'll rediscover your love of food and hopefully your oxalate symptoms will start to reduce. You might even start to introduce foods that previously weren't possible with the help of your practitioner.

So what's the deal with oxalates?

Embarking on the 30-day *Low-Oxalate Reset* can be a game-changer for individuals who are susceptible to kidney stones or suffer from certain gut issues. Oxalates are natural compounds found in various plant-based foods that can accumulate in the body, leading to the formation of kidney stones or contributing to gut-related problems. By reducing oxalate intake, the risk of kidney stone formation decreases, and gut health can improve.

Within 30 days of following a low-oxalate diet, one can expect to experience relief from symptoms, improved digestion, and a decreased likelihood of developing kidney stones. This dietary approach may also benefit individuals with autoimmune conditions or those who are sensitive to high-oxalate foods. By incorporating our meal plans and recipes, you can make an informed decision to adopt a low-oxalate diet and potentially improve your overall well-being.

On all of the above, we're confident that we've built on the success of our first title. As before, we've gathered the best and most trusted oxalate lists and guides from around the world, and combined them into one easy-to-digest *Low-Oxalate Reset*. And now, we've got even more to offer—think context around the oxalate diet, descriptions, meal plans, and a whole bunch of mouthwatering recipes.

Yes, going low oxalate doesn't have to be a struggle. Who even likes buckwheat groats and rice bran anyway?

Over the next 30 days, you'll embark on a transformative journey that will redefine your relationship with food. We understand that making dietary changes can be daunting, but our *Low-Oxalate Reset* is designed to make the transition as seamless as possible. With our carefully curated food list, delicious recipes, and lifestyle recommendations, you'll find everything you need to make low-oxalate eating a natural part of your life.

In this *Low-Oxalate Reset*, you'll learn about oxalates and their impact on your body. You'll discover how to identify foods that are high in oxalates and make smarter choices for your health. And most importantly, you'll enjoy a variety of delicious and nutritious low-oxalate meals and snacks that will leave you feeling satisfied and energized.

At the heart of our program is the belief that a low-oxalate lifestyle is a journey, not a destination. Our aim is to equip you with the knowledge, skills, and confidence you need to successfully navigate a low-oxalate diet and enjoy a lifetime of delicious and nutritious meals.

Join us on this empowering 30-day adventure and discover a world of incredible flavors, improved health, and newfound confidence in your low-oxalate transformation.

2. THE LOW-OXALATE LIFESTYLE: UNDERSTANDING THE BASICS

Strap in for as easy an explanation of oxalates as we can bring to you. These sneaky little compounds can make it tough for people to maintain a healthy diet, as they're present in so many common foods. In this chapter, we'll dive into what oxalates are and how they can affect your health.

So, let's start by understanding what our body does with oxalates. They're not essential for us, so they bind to other waste products in food and eventually make their way to the kidneys for excretion. Often, oxalates bind to minerals like calcium and are excreted from our body through urine and stool. However, consuming too many oxalates can prevent the body from flushing them out, which can lead to kidney stones.

You'll find oxalates in many plant-based foods, such as fruits, vegetables, nuts, and grains. While some are harmless and even beneficial, others can cause health problems, particularly for people who are prone to kidney stones or other oxalate-related health issues.

Did you know that our bodies create oxalates too? As we break down vitamin C molecules, oxalic acid is produced. Additionally, molds and yeast, like Aspergillus and Candida, can also be a source of oxalates in our diets. Therefore, it's essential to be mindful of our oxalate consumption and find a healthy balance that works for our unique bodies.

According to a research paper by the National Library of Medicine, there are significant variations in reported oxalate content in foods across multiple sources, which can make constructing a low-oxalate diet challenging. That's why we've created *Low-Oxalate Reset*. We've compiled the most reliable oxalate lists and guides to create a comprehensive food list that you can refer to throughout the program.

We've taken a unique approach to this *Low-Oxalate Reset* to make it the (we believe!) easiest low-oxalate program out there. We believe that a low-oxalate diet can be delicious and exciting, and with many scrumptious recipes in this book, we're confident that you'll rediscover your love of food and nourish your body at the same time.

We urge you to take things slowly and try ingredients carefully because everyone's body is different. When you try the recipes we share in this *Low-Oxalate Reset*, we hope you'll realize it's possible to still love food and see a reduction in your oxalate-related symptoms. You might even discover new foods that weren't possible before.

We think that food is one of life's great pleasures, and believe that a low-oxalate diet doesn't have to mean sacrificing taste or enjoyment. Our goal with *Low-Oxalate Reset* is to help you enjoy life and create delicious recipes that leave you feeling nourished, satisfied, and happy to eat them alone or with friends.

We've also ensured that our recipes use healthy and nourishing ingredients that are low in oxalates but also good for your body. For instance, we use coconut flour, which is lower in oxalates than other flours (coconut and oat flours are thought to be superior choices to some others which can be high or very high in oxalates). We want to ensure that you can enjoy delicious food without worrying about triggering your oxalate intolerance.

3. THE BENEFITS OF A LOW-OXALATE DIET FOR KIDNEY HEALTH AND OVERALL WELLBEING

Are you ready to dive into the world of low-oxalate living? In this chapter, we'll explore the benefits of a low-oxalate lifestyle and how it can help improve your overall health and wellbeing.

One of the most significant benefits of a low-oxalate diet is that it can help reduce the risk of kidney stones. Kidney stones can be horrible (to say the least). They are painful and disruptive to your daily life, so by limiting your oxalate intake, you can reduce the formation of new stones and prevent the recurrence of existing ones.

But that's not all. Studies have also suggested that reducing oxalate intake may improve symptoms in people with chronic pain, fibromyalgia, and other related conditions. So a low-oxalate lifestyle can also help with other health issues beyond kidney stones.

Another benefit of a low-oxalate diet is that it can promote gut health. High oxalate intake has been linked to gut inflammation and digestive problems, but by reducing your oxalate intake, you may experience less bloating, gas, and discomfort, allowing you to enjoy meals without discomfort.

Plus, a low-oxalate diet can support a healthy weight and reduce the risk of chronic diseases such as diabetes and heart disease. By focusing on nutrient-dense, low-oxalate foods, you can improve your overall nutrition and support healthy body weight management.

And here's some good news: following a low-oxalate lifestyle doesn't have to mean sacrificing taste or variety. By experimenting with new recipes and ingredients, you can discover new, delicious foods that you may not have tried before.

In summary, a low-oxalate lifestyle has many benefits, including reducing the risk of kidney stones, improving gut health, promoting a healthy weight, reducing the risk of chronic diseases, and discovering new, delicious foods.

In the next section we'll dive into the low-oxalate food list, exploring which foods to avoid and which ones are safe to eat on a low-oxalate diet. So let's continue on this transformative journey towards better health and wellbeing.

4. SHOPPING LIST: IDENTIFYING HIGH AND LOW OXALATE FOODS AND UNDERSTANDING PORTION SIZES

In our previous book, we listed out every low oxalate food and offered comments on each one. We gave it a score between 1 and 5 for oxalate levels. We did the research and compared notes from the best sources out there, so you knew you were getting reliable info. That meant no more confusion over serving sizes or mg per 100g - we simplified it all for you.

We're not going to do that here (as it took a whole book to do it previously!), but here are some simplified shopping lists for you, with precise details of why we allocated various foods to various categories.

- Low-Oxalate Shopping List: (Thought to be) 0–9 mg per serving
- Moderate-Oxalate Shopping List: (Thought to be) 10–25 mg per serving
- High-Oxalate Shopping List: (Thought to be) 26–99 mg per serving

A reminder, this is not a precise science. This book is a labor of love, but the major lists do disagree on oxalate content. As we've already said, consult with your practitioner before making any changes. Think of this as a helpful guide that can assist you on your journey, but you do need an expert to make this work properly.

Low oxalate foods:

Acerola

Alcohol
Algae
Anchovies
Apple
Apple cider vinegar
Apricot
Banana
Barley
Basil
Beef
Beer
Bison
Bivalves (mussels, oyster, clams, scallops)
Bok choi
Boysenberry
Brandy
Broad-leaved garlic
Butter
Cabbage
Cauliflower
Cep mushrooms
Chamomile and chamomile tea
Champagne
Cherry
Cheddar cheese
Cheese made from unpasteurized "raw" milk
Cheeses
Chicken
Chicory
Chives
Cilantro (Coriander)
Coconut and coconut derivatives
Cress
Coffee
Corn salad, lamb's lettuce
Cornflakes
Courgette
Crab
Cranberries and cranberry juice

Crawfish
Crayfish
Cream cheeses
Cream
Cucumber
Dextrose
Dill
Dried meat
Dry-cured meats
Duck
Egg white
Egg yolk
Endive
Espresso
Feta cheese
Fish
Game (meat)
Garlic
Goat's milk
Goose (organic, freshly cooked)
Gouda cheese
Grapes
Green peas
Ham (dried, cured)
Hemp seeds (Cannabis sativa)
Honey
Horseradish
Juniper berries
Kale
Kefir
Kohlrabi
Lamb
Lamb's lettuce, corn salad
Lard
Lentils
Lobster
Lychee
Lettuce
Liquor
Margarine
Marrow
Mascarpone cheese
Melon
Milk
Minced meat
Mint
Morello cherries
Mozzarella cheese
Mushrooms, different types
Mustard and mustard seeds
Napa cabbage
Nectarine
Nori seaweed
Oats
Olive oil
Onion

Ostrich
Oyster
Peach
Pear
Peas (green)
Papaya
Passion fruit
Peppermint tea
Plum
Pork
Poultry meat
Prawn
Processed cheese
Pumpkin
Rabbit
Raclette cheese
Radish
Raisins
Rice cakes
Rapeseed oil (called canola oil in US)
Raw milk
Red cabbage
Ricotta cheese
Rooibos tea
Roquefort cheese
Rosemary
Rum
Sage
Salami
Salmon
Sauerkraut
Sausages of all kinds
Savoy cabbage
Schnapps
Seafood
Seaweed
Sheep's milk, sheep milk
Shellfish
Shrimp
Smoked fish
Smoked meat
Snow peas
Soft cheese
Sour cream
Sparkling wine
Spirits
Strawberry
Sugar
Sunflower oil
Sunflower seeds
Thyme
Trout
Tuna
Turkey
Venison

Watermelon
White Rice
White button mushroom
Yogurt/Yoghurt
Zucchini/Courgette

Medium oxalate foods:

Artificial sweeteners
Asparagus
Bell pepper (sweet)
Blackberry
Blue cheeses
Blueberries
Broccoli
Brown Rice
Chickpeas
Chili pepper, red, fresh
Curry
Dates
Figs (fresh or dried)
Flaxseed (linseed)
Fructose (fruit sugar)
Herbal tea
Kelp
Lemon (but considered acceptable without peel)
Lime
Maltodextrin
Maple syrup
Nettle tea
Oregano
Pea Shoots (or pea sprouts)
Pumpkin seed oil
Pumpkin seeds
Red wine vinegar
Rice milk
Rice noodles
Spelt
Squashes
Stinging nettle
Sweetcorn
Wild rice
Wine

High oxalate foods:

Agave syrup
Almond
Artichokes
Aubergine
Avocado
Bamboo shoots
Barley malt, malt
Beans
Beetroot
Bell pepper (hot)
Blue fenugreek

Black caraway
Blackcurrants
Borlotti beans
Bouillon
Brazil nut
Bread
Broad beans
Brussels sprouts
Buckwheat
Cactus pear
Cardamom
Carrot
Cashew nut
Cassava
Celery
Chia, chia seeds
Chard
Chocolate
Cinnamon
Citrus fruits
Clover
Cloves
Cocoa butter and cacao butter
Cocoa drinks, powder, etc
Cumin
Dragon fruit
Elderflower cordial
Fennel
Fenugreek
Ginger
Goji berry
Gooseberry, gooseberries
Grapefruit
Green beans
Green tea
Guava
Hazelnut
Kiwi
Leek
Liquorice
Loganberry
Macadamia
Malt extract
Malt
Mandarin orange
Mango
Mate tea
Millet
Morel
Mulberry
Mungbeans (germinated, sprouting)
Nutmeg
Nuts (see individual nuts for more details)
Olives

Orange
Parsley
Parsnip
Peanuts
Pickled food
Pineapple
Pistachio
Pomegranate
Poppy seeds
Potato
Prune
Pulses
Quinoa
Raspberry
Redcurrants
Rhubarb
Rye
Sesame
Soy (soy beans, soy flour)
Soy sauce
Spinach
Stevia
Sweet potato
Tea, black
Tomato
Turmeric
Turnip
Vanilla
Vinegar: balsamic
Vinegar: distilled white vinegar
Walnut
Watercress
Wheat
Wheat germ
Yam
Yeast

Keep in mind that a low-oxalate diet is highly individual, and our sources vary significantly. When trying new foods, proceed with caution.

Again, this book and this list should not be used to replace any form of medicine or professional medical advice. The information provided is solely for educational and entertainment purposes. Always ask your doctor before starting a new diet.

5. TIPS FOR TRANSITIONING TO A LOW-OXALATE LIFESTYLE

Are you ready to embark on a journey towards a healthier low-oxalate lifestyle? Transitioning to a low-oxalate diet can seem daunting at first, but with the right mindset and some practical tips, it can be a fun and rewarding experience. Whether you're doing this for health reasons or just curious to try something new, you're in for a treat! In this section, we'll share some basic pointers to make your transition to a low-oxalate lifestyle as smooth and enjoyable as possible.

1. Take it one step at a time: Yes yes, we know this seems obvious, but we really mean it here. Transitioning to a low-oxalate lifestyle can be overwhelming and take your body some time to adjust, so it's important to take it slow. Don't go all in (however tempting that is). Start by eliminating a few high-oxalate foods at a time and gradually work your way up.
2. Experiment with new (low-oxalate) foods: Trying new foods and recipes can be exciting and help you discover new low-oxalate options. Don't be afraid to experiment and get creative in the kitchen, as always with the assistance of your practitioner to ease the low-oxalate transition.

3. Plan ahead: Planning your meals and snacks in advance can help you stay on track and avoid reaching for high-oxalate foods when you're hungry and unprepared. We are those people who take big tupperwares out of low oxalate snacks so we don't get caught hungry out and about.
4. Stay hydrated: Drinking plenty of water can help prevent kidney stone formation and support overall health. Aim for at least 8 glasses of water a day.
5. Seek support: Did we already mention it's worth getting a good practitioner? Making dietary changes can be challenging, so don't be afraid to seek support from a healthcare professional. Joining a support group or online community can also be helpful. And make sure your family and friends are on board, there's nothing worse than them cooking up a big meal with spinach and rhubarb, then insisting you'll be fine!)
6. Don't beat yourself up: Stay optimistic - who even likes spinach and rhubarb anyway? You've still got loads of low oxalate alternatives.

Remember, transitioning to a low-oxalate lifestyle is a journey, and it's important to take it one day at a time. With time, patience, and support, you can successfully adopt a low-oxalate lifestyle and improve your health and wellbeing.

6. STUDIES AND RESEARCH SUPPORTING LOW-OXALATE DIETS

Emerging and established science and research shows that a low-oxalate diet can have some excellent benefits for your overall health and wellbeing.

1. A National Health and Nutrition Examination Survey carried out in the USA between 2007 & 2010 suggests that kidney stones affect 1 in 11 people.
2. The National Institute of Diabetes and Digestive and Kidney Diseases in the USA suggests that eating more low oxalate foods can help reduce oxalates in your urine and therefore reduce your risk of oxalate kidney stones.
3. Urology of Virginia has a very interesting and slightly alarming report about the damaging effects on the human body of oxalates. It says, 'If you're eating a lot of high-oxalate foods and are struggling with any kind of chronic health issue that doesn't seem to respond to other sensible lifestyle changes and treatments, you'd be wise to give a low- or no-oxalate diet a try.'
4. The American Journal of Gastroenterology has a case study in 2020 of a woman with multiple health issues who changed to a low oxalate diet and saw a significant improvement.

https://www.ncbi.nlm.nih.gov/pmc/articles/PMC3362665/

https://www.niddk.nih.gov/health-information/urologic-diseases/kidney-stones/eating-diet-nutrition

https://www.urologyofva.net/articles/category/healthy-living/3740469/11/13/2019/the-damaging-effects-of-oxalates-on-the-human-body/&sa=D&source=docs&ust=1681976684805141&usg=AOvVaw0dn9Ur9-Fr62aN_DT0Q1kg

https://journals.lww.com/ajg/fulltext/2020/10001/s2047_beware_of_nuts_and_seeds__a_case_of_high.2047.aspx&sa=D&source=docs&ust=1681976684799061&usg=AOvVaw27y2QQOt-Zxyy26NzYZhZH9

These are just some of the studies we are impressed by for a low oxalate. Let's first focus on those kidney stones we mentioned previously. If you've ever had one, you know they're no joke. They're painful, and they can even lead to serious complications. The good news is that studies have found that a low-oxalate diet can help prevent kidney stones from forming in the first place. That's because oxalate is one of the main components of most kidney stones, so by reducing your oxalate intake, you're reducing your risk of developing stones.

But that's not all. Some research has also linked high oxalate intake to other health issues, such as inflammation and oxidative stress. Oxidative stress is a fancy term for when there are too many harmful molecules called free radicals in your body, and not enough antioxidants to neutralize them. Over time, this can cause damage to your cells and contribute to the development of chronic diseases like heart disease, cancer, and Alzheimer's. By following a low-oxalate diet, you can reduce your risk of oxidative stress and inflammation.

Now, you might be wondering, "But aren't some high-oxalate foods really good for you?" And the answer is well, potentially. Spinach, for example, is packed with nutrients like iron and vitamin K. But it is one of the highest oxalate foods in the world. We can find alternatives quite easily that don't pack so many oxalates into a tiny space.

You may or may not need to cut out all high-oxalate foods completely depending on the treatment program you are on. However if you are following our *Low-Oxalate Reset*, you just need to be mindful of how much you're consuming and make sure you're getting a variety of other nutrient-dense foods as well.

Overall, the science behind low-oxalate diets is compelling. By reducing your intake of high oxalate foods, you can decrease inflammation in your body, which can lead to a whole host of positive changes. And, by incorporating more low-oxalate fruits and veggies, you're getting a healthy dose of vitamins and minerals that can help support gut health.

And research has even shown that a low-oxalate diet may help improve symptoms of inflammatory bowel disease (IBD) and other digestive disorders. Plus, by cutting back on high oxalate foods like processed snacks and sugary treats, you're also reducing your intake of other unhealthy ingredients like refined sugars and unhealthy fats. All in all, transitioning to a low-oxalate lifestyle can have a positive impact on both your physical and mental health.

These studies above and others suggest that a low-oxalate diet can have a range of health benefits and may be particularly helpful for individuals with specific health conditions, such as kidney stones, chronic kidney disease, inflammation, and IBS.

PART TWO

THE LOW-OXALATE RESET: YOUR 30-DAY ROADMAP TO SUCCESS

7. STOCKING YOUR LOW-OXALATE PANTRY: ESSENTIAL INGREDIENTS AND MORE SHOPPING TIPS

We've already explored which ingredients are low oxalate in our shopping list section, and now let's stock your low-oxalate kitchen with what we consider to be some essentials:

1. Fresh Vegetables: Vegetables are an essential part of any healthy diet, and they're particularly important when following a low-oxalate diet. Some of the best low-oxalate vegetables include lettuce, cauliflower, cabbage, endive, and bok choy. Obviously there are some big ones to avoid (hello, spinach), and the details are in the food and shopping lists elsewhere in this book.
2. Fresh Fruits: Some of the best low-oxalate fruits include apples, pears, peaches, cherries, and bananas.
3. Lean Proteins: Protein is an essential nutrient for building and repairing tissues, and it's particularly important when following a low-oxalate diet. Some of the best low-oxalate protein sources include chicken, turkey, fish, and eggs.
4. Whole Grains: Whole grains are an important source of fiber and other essential nutrients, and they're also a good option when following a low-oxalate diet. Some of

the best low-oxalate grains include white rice, spelt and sorghum.

5. Dairy Products: Dairy products are a good source of calcium and other essential nutrients, and they're also low in oxalates. Some of the best low-oxalate dairy products include milk, cheese, and yogurt.

Label Tips for a Low-Oxalate Pantry

When shopping for packaged foods, always read the labels carefully to check for high oxalate ingredients. This sounds obvious, but our low-oxalate lifestyle often falls down because we haven't checked the ingredients properly.

Some common high-oxalate ingredients to watch out for include spinach, rhubarb, beets, almonds, and cocoa powder (which appears in a lot of store-bought bars and so on). Beet powder is often used to color foods, and almonds appear in a lot of low-carb and keto items.

8. MASTERING THE ART OF LOW-OXALATE COOKING: TECHNIQUES AND HACKS

Soaking and sprouting

Soaking and sprouting are two great techniques that can help reduce oxalate levels in grains, legumes, and nuts while making them easier to digest.

Soaking involves soaking the ingredient in water for several hours or overnight, while sprouting involves soaking and allowing the ingredient to sprout over several days.

Yes, it takes some extra time, but it's worth it for those on a low-oxalate diet! It considerably reduces the oxalate content and makes the food more digestible.

When you sprout grains like oats, some cool things happen on a scientific level. The process breaks down the not-so-friendly compounds, including oxalates, and makes it easier for your body to absorb all the good stuff.

During sprouting, enzyme activity kicks into high gear, and the oats go through a sort of "pre-digestion" process. This means that nutrients become more available and easier to absorb, while at the same time, the oxalate content drops. It's a win-win situation for low oxalate dieters.

In addition you can buy plenty of sprouted products in the shops. We particularly like buying sprouted oats, although they tend to be a bit more expensive. If you are somebody who can tolerate medium-oxalate foods, then sprouted flaxseed is freely available in the shops too.

But what about the flavor?

Low-oxalate herbs and spices like basil, oregano, thyme, and turmeric can add bold flavors to dishes. Don't forget about healthy fats like avocado oil and coconut oil for richness and depth, and citrus fruits like lemon and lime for brightness and acidity. Mixing and matching different flavor combinations can lead to some seriously tasty low-oxalate meals.

Certain cooking techniques can also help reduce oxalate levels in foods. Blanching and boiling can help remove some of the oxalate from veggies like broccoli and cauliflower, while roasting and grilling can be effective for other ingredients. Be careful not to overcook though, as this can destroy valuable nutrients.

Stocking a low-oxalate kitchen needn't be a challenge, and keeping a list of go-to low-oxalate ingredients on hand can help with meal planning and grocery shopping.

A high-quality blender and food processor are also useful for creating low-oxalate smoothies, sauces, and dips. Lastly, keeping a variety of low-oxalate snacks on hand, like fresh fruit and veggies, can help prevent cravings and keep hunger at bay.

9. DINING OUT AND SOCIALIZING ON A LOW-OXALATE DIET

Are you worried about dining out or socializing on a low-oxalate diet? We'll be honest, it's not always straightforward. Some advance research is sometimes needed. And most of the time you'll probably be following the meal plan and recipes at home. But, here are some tips and tricks to help you navigate these situations like a low-oxalate pro.

1. Do Your Research:

Before heading out, do some research on the restaurant or venue you're going to. Check out their menu online and see if they have any low-oxalate options available. If not, consider calling ahead and asking the restaurant if they can make modifications to a dish to make it low-oxalate. Yes we have done that before. If you are like us you may not want to do this, but at the very least, we do ask for the 'salmon without the spinach' for example once we get to the restaurant. Talking of which...

2. Customize Your Order

Don't be afraid to ask for modifications to a dish to make it low-oxalate. For example, if a salad contains high-oxalate ingredients like spinach or almonds, ask if they can substitute with low-oxalate alternatives. Most restaurants are willing to accommodate dietary restrictions, so don't be shy about asking for what you need.

3. Avoid Hidden Oxalates

Sauces and dressings can be a hidden source of oxalate, so it's important to be mindful of what you're adding to your dish.

4. Choose Your Drinks Carefully

A friend of ours often loudly declares that he is 'gluten-free', and then pours himself a large beer (with gluten in it). Drinks are a place we often come unstuck with different diets. Many popular drinks like draft and dark beers, turmeric latte and green tea can be high in oxalate as can smoothies made with beets, orange juice or spinach.

10. TIPS FOR STAYING MOTIVATED AND ACCOUNTABLE ON YOUR LOW-OXALATE JOURNEY

Embarking on a low-oxalate diet can be a challenging journey, but don't worry, we've got your back! Here are some tips to help you stay motivated and accountable:

1. Keep a low-oxalate food diary: Keeping a food diary can help you stay accountable and track your progress. Write down everything you eat and drink, including the oxalate content, and review it regularly to see how you're doing. One of the reasons we particularly like this and believe it is important is that people react differently to ingredients, so you have to figure out what suits you. Also - the aim is after a while you will be transitioning back to a more 'normal diet' and this helps you consult where you are at in your journey.
2. Find a support system: Having a support system can be crucial to staying motivated. Join a low-oxalate support group or find a friend who is also following a low-oxalate diet. Share your challenges and successes with each other.

3. Get creative in the kitchen: Eating a low-oxalate diet doesn't mean you have to eat bland food. Get creative in the kitchen and experiment with new recipes and ingredients. You may be surprised at how delicious low-oxalate meals can be.
4. Be prepared: One of the biggest challenges of following a low-oxalate diet is finding suitable options when eating out or traveling. Be prepared by packing snacks and researching restaurants in advance to ensure there are low-oxalate options available.
5. Practice self-care: Don't forget to take care of yourself beyond just following a low-oxalate diet. Make time for self-care activities like exercise, meditation, and spending time with loved ones.
6. Celebrate your successes: Finally, celebrate your successes, no matter how small they may seem. Recognize and acknowledge your progress and use it as motivation to keep going

PART THREE

RESET MEAL PLAN AND RECIPES: EATING WELL AND STARTING TO HEAL

11. YOUR LOW-OXALATE MEAL PLAN

Here is your 30-day meal plan for *Low-Oxalate Reset*. Feel free to mix and match days, ingredients and dishes. The idea is simply to go lower oxalate with these delicious recipes. We're not trying to hit a calorie count, carb count, or macro quota. We just want to go low oxalate, so this is a sample meal plan that you can adapt to your own taste.

In addition, feel free to miss breakfast if you are, for instance, a fan of intermittent fasting and would rather skip a morning meal or a snack.

Don't be afraid to tweak the ingredients a bit to make them your own. Whether you're vegetarian, vegan, or have any other dietary requirements, you can adapt these recipes to suit your needs. Not a fan of Slow-Cooked Beef Shin, or vegetarian? Fine, sub in something else for dinner like Veggie Tray Bake with Cheese and Honey.

30-Day Low-Oxalate Meal Plan

Week 1:

Monday:

- Breakfast: Fruity Fusion Breakfast with Delicious Toppings

- Snack: Crispy Kohlrabi and Apple Chips
- Lunch: Pumpkin Soup
- Dinner: Tender Slow-Cooked Beef
- Dessert: Flippin' Lovely Coconut Pancakes

Tuesday:

- Breakfast: Yummy Honey Granola
- Snack: Crispy Crackers with Sunflower Butter Spread
- Lunch: Fruit and Fibre Soup
- Dinner: Succulent Pork Burger Bites
- Dessert: Quick Strawberries and Cream Delight

Wednesday:

- Breakfast: Spiced Pumpkin Oatmeal
- Snack: Low-oxalate fruit (check our list)
- Lunch: Savory Cheese and Peas
- Dinner: Baked Veg and Cheese with Maple Syrup
- Dessert: Simple Oat Bars

Thursday:

- Breakfast: Sunrise Strawberry Smoothie
- Snack: Grab 'n Go Snacks
- Lunch: Yummy Chicken Salad
- Dinner: Cauliflower Rice Thai Style
- Dessert: Refreshing Lemon and Watermelon "Ice Cream"

Friday:

- Breakfast: Green Smoothie
- Snack: Crispy Crackers with Sunflower Spread
- Lunch: Piperade Omelet
- Dinner: Prawn and Broccoli Stir Fry
- Dessert: Flippin' Lovely Coconut Pancakes

Saturday:

- Breakfast: Creamy Banana and Blueberry Smoothie
- Snack: Low-oxalate fruit (check our list)
- Lunch: Veggie Soup with Rice
- Dinner: Baked Lemon Dill Salmon
- Dessert: Quick Strawberries and Cream Delight

Sunday:

- Breakfast: Sage Infused Bulletproof Coffee and a bowl of cornflakes
- Snack: Crispy Kohlrabi and Apple Chips
- Lunch: Kale Delight Soup
- Dinner: Kohlrabi and Tofu Stir Fry
- Dessert: Simple Oat Bars

Week 2:

Monday:

- Breakfast: Peach-Cherry Yogurt Delight

- Snack: Grab 'n Go Snacks
- Lunch: Kale Delight Soup
- Dinner: Baked Lemon Dill Salmon
- Dessert: Quick Strawberries and Cream Delight

Tuesday:

- Breakfast: Coconut Craving Granola
- Snack: Crispy Kohlrabi and Apple Chips
- Lunch: Savory Mushroom and Sage Soup
- Dinner: Kohlrabi and Tofu Stir Fry
- Dessert: Flippin' Lovely Coconut Pancakes

Wednesday:

- Breakfast: Creamy Banana and Blueberry Smoothie
- Snack: Low-oxalate fruit (check our list)
- Lunch: Piperade Omelet
- Dinner: Tender Slow-Cooked Beef
- Dessert: Simple Oat Bars

Thursday:

- Breakfast: Sage Infused Bulletproof Coffee and Rice cereal
- Snack: Crispy Crackers with Sunflower Spread
- Lunch: Fruit and Fibre Soup
- Dinner: Succulent Pork Burger Bites
- Dessert: Refreshing Lemon and Watermelon "Ice Cream"

Friday:

- Breakfast: Wholesome Breakfast Flatbread
- Snack: Crispy Kohlrabi and Apple Chips
- Lunch: Savory Cheese and Peas
- Dinner: Baked Veg and Cheese with Maple Syrup
- Dessert: Flippin' Lovely Coconut Pancakes

Saturday:

- Breakfast: Fruity Fusion Breakfast with Delicious Toppings
- Snack: Low-oxalate fruit (check our list)
- Lunch: Yummy Chicken Salad
- Dinner: Prawn and Broccoli Stir Fry
- Dessert: Quick Strawberries and Cream Delight

Sunday:

- Breakfast: Sunrise Strawberry Smoothie
- Snack: Grab 'n Go Snacks
- Lunch: Veggie Soup with Rice
- Dinner: Cauliflower Rice Thai Style
- Dessert: Simple Oat Bars

Week 3:

Monday:

- Breakfast: Tropical Papaya Smoothie
- Snack: Crispy Crackers with Sunflower Spread

- Lunch: Kale Delight Soup
- Dinner: Succulent Pork Burger Bites
- Dessert: Refreshing Lemon and Watermelon "Ice Cream"

Tuesday:

- Breakfast: Yummy Honey Granola
- Snack: Crispy Kohlrabi and Apple Chips
- Lunch: Pumpkin Soup
- Dinner: Baked Lemon Dill Salmon
- Dessert: Flippin' Lovely Coconut Pancakes

Wednesday:

- Breakfast: Fruity Yogurt Breakfast
- Snack: Low-oxalate fruit (check our list)
- Lunch: Fruit and Fibre Soup
- Dinner: Cauliflower Rice Thai Style
- Dessert: Quick Strawberries and Cream Delight

Thursday:

- Breakfast: Coconut Craving Granola
- Snack: Grab 'n Go Snacks
- Lunch: Savory Cheese and Peas
- Dinner: Kohlrabi and Tofu Stir Fry
- Dessert: Simple Oat Bars

Friday:

- Breakfast: Fruity Fusion Breakfast with Delicious Toppings
- Snack: Crispy Crackers with Sunflower Spread
- Lunch: Yummy Chicken Salad
- Dinner: Baked Veg and Cheese with Maple Syrup
- Dessert: Refreshing Lemon and Watermelon "Ice Cream"

Saturday:

- Breakfast: Yummy Honey Granola
- Snack: Low-oxalate fruit (check our list)
- Lunch: Veggie Soup with Rice
- Dinner: Tender Slow-Cooked Beef
- Dessert: Flippin' Lovely Coconut Pancakes

Sunday:

- Breakfast: Spiced Pumpkin Oatmeal
- Snack: Crispy Kohlrabi and Apple Chips
- Lunch: Kale Delight Soup
- Dinner: Prawn and Broccoli Stir Fry
- Dessert: Quick Strawberries and Cream Delight

Week 4:

Monday:

- Breakfast: Sunrise Strawberry Smoothie
- Snack: Crispy Crackers with Sunflower Spread
- Lunch: Refreshing Lettuce and Pea Soup
- Dinner: Prawn and Broccoli Stir Fry

- Dessert: Simple Oat Bars

Tuesday:

- Breakfast: Green Smoothie
- Snack: Low-oxalate fruit (check our list)
- Lunch: Savory Mushroom and Sage Soup
- Dinner: Baked Lemon Dill Salmon
- Dessert: Refreshing Lemon and Watermelon "Ice Cream"

Wednesday:

- Breakfast: Creamy Banana and Blueberry Smoothie
- Snack: Crispy Kohlrabi and Apple Chips
- Lunch: Pumpkin Soup
- Dinner: Kohlrabi and Tofu Stir Fry
- Dessert: Flippin' Lovely Coconut Pancakes

Thursday:

- Breakfast: Sage Infused Bulletproof Coffee and Rice cereal
- Snack: Grab 'n Go Snacks
- Lunch: Fruit and Fibre Soup
- Dinner: Cauliflower Rice Thai Style
- Dessert: Quick Strawberries and Cream Delight

Friday:

- Breakfast: Peach-Cherry Yogurt Delight
- Snack: Crispy Crackers with Sunflower Spread

- Lunch: Savory Cheese and Peas
- Dinner: Tender Slow-Cooked Beef
- Dessert: Flippin' Lovely Coconut Pancakes

Saturday:

- Breakfast: Wholesome Breakfast Flatbread
- Snack: Low-oxalate fruit (check our list)
- Lunch: Yummy Chicken Salad
- Dinner: Baked Veg and Cheese with Maple Syrup
- Dessert: Simple Oat Bars

Sunday:

- Breakfast: Coconut Craving Granola
- Snack: Crispy Kohlrabi and Apple Chips
- Lunch: Veggie Soup with Rice
- Dinner: Succulent Pork Burger Bites
- Dessert: Refreshing Lemon and Watermelon "Ice Cream"

This super-flexible meal plan is packed with delicious low-oxalate meals that you can mix and match as you like. Feel free to play around with the order of dishes, swap them out for other low-oxalate recipes, or even go wild and have smoothies and pancakes for breakfast! Just make sure to chat with a healthcare professional or nutritionist if you're unsure about anything related to your diet or specific health needs. Have fun and enjoy your tasty low-oxalate adventure!

12. DELICIOUS AND NUTRITIOUS LOW-OXALATE RECIPES

This section of the book is devoted to helping you cook delicious low-oxalate recipes over the next 30 days. You want to go low oxalate but you aren't sure about what to eat? You're in the right place. For this part of the book we are delighted to have partnered with The Low Oxalate Cookbook to adapt some of their recipes and take all new vibrant pictures too. Please note that the nutritional values provided are approximate and can vary based on ingredients and proportions.

As always, consult your practitioner before starting any new diet or regime. (Yes, we keep emphasizing that fact, but it's important. Your oxalate issues might be different from the next person, so it's always best to check.)

★ Yummy Honey Granola

Feast your eyes on this scrumptious treat. Our low-oxalate granola is so yummy, it's gobbled up in no time!

Serves 2.

Ingredients:

2 cups gluten-free oats
3 tbsp. sunflower seeds
3 tbsp. coconut flakes
2 tbsp. coconut oil
¼ cup honey
Few strawberries
Dollop of yogurt

Instructions:

1. Preheat your oven to 300°F (150°C).
2. In a large mixing bowl, chuck in the oats, sunflower seeds, and coconut flakes.
3. Melt the coconut oil in a small saucepan or in the microwave, and then add it to the dry ingredients.
4. Pour in the honey and stir until everything is well coated.
5. Spread the mixture evenly on a baking sheet lined with parchment paper.
6. Bake for 15-20 minutes, or until the granola is golden brown and crispy. Keep an eye on it as it can easily burn.
7. Allow the granola to cool completely before serving or storing in an airtight container.
8. Serve with some lush strawberries and a dollop of natural yogurt.

Nutritional Values Per Serving:

Calories: 276 kcal
Carbohydrates: 33.2g
Dietary Fiber: 3.5g
Protein: 4.75g
Fat: 15g

★ Fruity Fusion Breakfast with Delicious Toppings

Kick-start your day with these delightful Fruity Fusion bakes, perfect for treating the whole family. Each one is unique with a variety of fun toppings. Why not invent your own toppings, really go wild!

Serves 4 bowls

Ingredients:

FOR THE FRUITY FUSION BAKES:

1 cup cream cheese or desiccated coconut
1 cup milk
2 eggs
1 cup fresh/frozen strawberries
1 cup fresh/frozen raspberries
2 tbsp butter
2 tbsp. honey

FOR THE TOPPINGS:

2 tbsp. cream
1 tbsp. chia seeds
1 tbsp sliced strawberries

OPTIONAL:

1 tbsp. fresh blackberries
1 tbsp. honey
1 tbsp coconut flakes

Instructions:

1. Preheat the oven to 180°C (350°F) and grab a baking dish.
2. Whip the eggs and butter together. Combine all the ingredients for the bakes in a dish or 6-8 individual pots and mix well. Bake for about 30-40 minutes or (15-25 minutes for the pots); turning halfway through.
3. Allow to cool after removing from the oven.
4. Add your choice of low oxalate toppings and munch away!

Nutritional Values Per Serving

Calories: 314 kcal
Protein: 10.5g
Carbohydrates: 23.5g
Fat: 16.8g
Dietary Fiber: 1.9g

★ Spiced Pumpkin Oatmeal

We're kicking off your day with some delightful low-oxalate goodness. Keep in mind that we've used milk in this and several other recipes. Dairy works well for the oxalate diet, but you might want to avoid it if you have multiple intolerances.

Serves 1 medium bowl

Ingredients:

½ cup gluten-free oats
½ cup pumpkin puree
1 tbsp. honey
1 tbsp. sunflower seeds
1 cup milk
½ tsp. cinnamon
Optional Toppings: Apple or pear pieces

Instructions:

1. In a saucepan, cook pumpkin puree, milk, oats, and cinnamon over medium heat for about 8 minutes, stirring frequently.
2. Add or reduce milk to achieve your desired consistency.
3. Serve in a bowl, drizzle with honey, and finish with your preferred toppings.

Nutritional Values Per Serving

Calories: 310 kcal
Carbohydrates: 50g
Dietary Fiber: 9.4g
Protein: 18.6g
Fat: 8.5g

★ Sunrise Strawberry Smoothie

Indulge in a delightful combination of hemp seeds, sunflower seeds, and strawberries for an energizing low-oxalate breakfast. Consider choosing organic honey as a kitchen staple to reduce exposure to pesticides and support the environmental importance of bees.

Serves 2 smoothie glasses

Ingredients:

¼ cup sunflower seeds
2 cups oat milk, non-dairy
1 small squirt of honey (organic, if possible)
¾ cup fresh strawberries, chopped
1 tbsp. hemp seeds

Instructions:

1. In a blender, combine the strawberries, sunflower seeds, oat milk, honey, and hemp seeds. We always like to soak our seeds first for half an hour so you can always prepare a batch the night before. This helps reduce oxalic acid.
2. Blend until smooth.
3. Pour into glasses and enjoy.

Nutritional Values Per Serving

Calories: 301 cal
Carbohydrates: 22.3g
Dietary Fiber: 3g
Protein: 12.6g
Fat: 17.4g

★ Creamy Banana and Blueberry Smoothie

Serves 1

Yes it's simple, but therein lies the magic - we are on a mission to make this a simple transition for you. If it seems too easy, that's by design. We are trying to make the low-oxalate adjustment straightforward with a range of recipes.

Ingredients:

One small banana
Handful of fresh or frozen blueberries (about a half cup)
1/2 cup of your milk of choice (dairy, hemp or coconut) or water
2 tsp Flax seeds (optional)

Instructions

1. Chuck everything into your blender and wizz up until smooth. That's it.

Nutritional Values Per Serving:

Calories: 102 kcal
Carbohydrates: 16g
Dietary Fiber: 0.6g
Protein: 3g
Fat: 3g

★ Sage Infused Bulletproof Coffee

Wait, these ingredients are right? Yep, bear with us. This unusual blend supports intermittent fasting in the low-oxalate community, offering a satisfying, high-fat, and healthy start to the day without blood sugar spikes. Give it a try if you are into intermittent fasting or fasting alongside your low-oxalate lifestyle. (We have put this in the meal plan but offered a simple 'cornflakes' alternative as we do realize not everybody loves Sage Infused Bulletproof Coffee - but we do!)

Serves 1.

Ingredients:

Ground organic coffee
1 tsp coconut oil
1 tsp butter or ghee
A few sprigs of sage

Instructions:

1. Brew your coffee in your preferred way. We like to use a cafetière.
2. Add the sage sprigs to the cafetière, allowing the magic to happen as the sage is infused.
3. Once the sage coffee infusion is ready, remove the sprigs, add the coconut oil and butter, and blend until smooth.
4. Pour into your coffee mug and enjoy.

Nutritional Values Per Serving:

- Calories: 72kcal
- Carbohydrates: 0g
- Dietary Fiber: 0g
- Protein: 0.3g
- Fat: 8.3g

★ Green Smoothie

Boost your super powers with a green smoothie featuring kale, a low-oxalate and nutrient-packed ingredient. Enjoy this healthy and delicious drink in just a few easy steps.

Serves 2 glasses

Ingredients:

1 cup water (or more)
1 handful kale, torn
1 cup cucumber, diced
1 cup lettuce, diced
1 medium apple, sliced
2 tbsp. fresh or frozen cranberries

Instructions:

1. Combine all ingredients in a blender. Frozen cranberries will create a pleasing consistency.
2. Blend until smooth.

Nutritional Values Per Serving

Calories: 70 kcal
Carbohydrates: 16.3g
Dietary Fiber: 3.6g
Protein: 1.3g
Fat: 0.4g

★ Tropical Papaya Smoothie

Papaya, a remarkable low-oxalate ingredient, is the star of this smoothie. Though it may require extra effort to find, its unique taste is worth it.

Serves 1: 240 ml to 300 ml

Ingredients:

1 cup pitted papaya
¼ cup gluten-free oats
½ cup strawberries
½ -¾ cup coconut or regular milk
1 tbsp coconut flakes
Ice cubes

Instructions:

1. Combine all ingredients in a high-powered blender.
2. Blend, adding more milk if needed.
3. Enjoy your refreshing tropical papaya smoothie.

Nutritional Values Per Serving:

- Calories: 265 kcal
- Carbohydrates: 49.6g
- Dietary Fiber: 9.7g
- Protein: 9.8g
- Fat: 6.3g

★ Wholesome Breakfast Flatbread

Try this innovative and tasty low-oxalate breakfast option that's perfect for the whole family.

Serves 2 (one half is one serving)

Ingredients:

3 tbsp. hemp seeds
3 tbsp. sunflower seeds
1 cup oats
2 tsp. coconut sugar
2 tbsp. Low-Oxalate Sunflower Butter (see recipe)
1 tsp. butter
1 tsp. olive oil
Cranberry and yogurt, to taste

Instructions:

1. Soak the seeds in ½ cup of water for 30 minutes or longer, as soaking is beneficial for a low-oxalate diet. You'll see we do this on other recipes too.
2. Preheat the oven to 180°C (350°F) and prepare a baking sheet.
3. In a separate bowl, mix the Low-Oxalate Sunflower Butter, oats, honey, cinnamon, and olive oil. Chop the soaked seeds and add them to the mixture. Stir well to combine.
4. Spread the mixture evenly onto the baking sheet.
5. Bake for about 30 minutes or until the crust turns golden but not burnt.

Nutritional Values Per Serving

- Calories: 331 kcal
- Carbohydrates: 23g
- Dietary Fiber: 6.7g
- Protein: 10.6g
- Fat: 22.6g

★ Fruity Yogurt Breakfast

Enjoy a vibrant and fruity breakfast that's low-oxalate and easy to prepare. Adjust the sweetness by adding honey to your taste preference, though we recommend a lower sugar, lower carb diet for gut health.

Serves 1

Ingredients:

1/4 cup chopped peach
1/2 cup cherries
1/2 cup yogurt
1 tbsp raisins as a topping

Instructions:

1. Cut the cherries and chop the peach. Gently warm the fruits in a saucepan over low heat for 3-4 minutes to release their juices.
2. Allow the fruit mixture to cool before adding it to a mason jar along with honey and yogurt. Mix well.
3. Refrigerate the yogurt mixture for as long as you can resist eating it!
4. When ready to serve, top with raisins and enjoy.

Nutritional Values Per Serving:

- Calories: 189 kcal
- Carbohydrates: 33.5g
- Dietary Fiber: 2.8g
- Protein: 5.5g
- Fat: 4.1g

★ Coconut Craving Granola

Embrace the versatility of coconut in this granola, featuring both coconut flakes and desiccated coconut. Low-carb, low-histamine, and of course low-oxalate, this granola is perfect for various diets.

Serves 2 bowls

Ingredients:

- 1 cup oats
- 1 tbsp sunflower seeds
- 1 tbsp coconut flakes
- 2 tbsp coconut oil
- 1 tbsp desiccated coconut
- 1/4 tsp Himalayan salt
- 2 tsp of honey
- OPTIONAL: 1/2 tsp cinnamon

Toppings:

- OPTIONAL: 2 tbsp dried cranberries or dried apricots
- OPTIONAL: 2 tbsp organic coconut cream

Instructions:

1. Preheat the oven to 150°C (275°F) and prepare a baking tray.
2. Mix the dry ingredients, excluding the coconut flakes, in a bowl
3. Incorporate the wet ingredients and mix well.
4. Spread the mixture evenly on the baking tray.
5. Bake for 15 minutes, stirring frequently and monitoring closely.
6. Time for some coconut love. Add the coconut flakes and bake for a couple more minutes.
7. Your low-oxalate Coconut Craving Granola is ready to enjoy, just add your favorite topping.

Nutritional Values Per Serving:

- Calories: 292 kcal
- Carbohydrates: 32.3g
- Dietary Fiber: 4.1g
- Protein: 5.5g
- Fat: 17.8g

★ Crispy Kohlrabi and Apple Chips

Indulge in a delicious and nutritious low-oxalate snack with these crispy kohlrabi and apple chips. For extra crispiness, use a baking sheet with tiny holes in it.

Serves 1 large bowl

Ingredients:

2 apples, thinly sliced
2 large kohlrabi, thinly sliced
1 tbsp. extra-virgin olive oil
1 tsp. dried tarragon
Himalayan salt, to taste

Instructions:

1. Preheat the oven to 210°C (410°F) and line a baking sheet with foil. (You can also use an air fryer, but check every few minutes to avoid overcooking).
2. Spread the apple and kohlrabi slices on the sheet.
3. Bake until they are nicely browned, which may take about 20 minutes. Remove from the oven and let cool for at least 10 minutes or enjoy them right away.

Nutritional Values Per Serving

- Calories: 312 kcal
- Carbohydrates: 58g
- Dietary Fiber: 12.2g
- Protein: 6.9g
- Fat: 3.6g

★ Crispy Crackers

We're crackers for these sunflower seed crackers. They're perfect for enjoying with your favorite low-oxalate spreads or cheeses. So we took a picture of them alongside some sunflowers.

Makes 8 small crackers

Ingredients:

¾ cup oats
½ cup sunflower seeds
2 tbsp. hemp seeds
½ cup water
1 tsp.herbs de provence

Instructions:

1. Preheat the oven to 180°C (350°F) and line a baking tray with parchment paper.
2. In a bowl, mix all the ingredients until well combined and moist. Add a touch of water if too dry. You can add honey for sweetness if desired. Let the mixture sit for 30 minutes.
3. Spread the mixture evenly on the baking tray.
4. Bake for 20-30 minutes, keeping an eye on it to avoid burning. Flip and bake for another 10-15 minutes.
5. Remove from the oven and enjoy with your favorite low-oxalate toppings.

Nutritional Values Per Serving (1 cracker)

- Calories: 90kcal
- Carbohydrates: 12.4g
- Dietary Fiber: 2.6g
- Protein: 4g
- Fat: 5g

★ Sunflower Spread

Indulge in this rich and tasty sunflower butter, perfect for enjoying with your favorite low-oxalate snacks.

Serves 1 jar

Ingredients:

1 cup sunflower seeds
2 tbsp. coconut or olive oil

Instructions:

1. Soak sunflower seeds in filtered water for at least 30 minutes to remove oxalic acid.
2. Preheat the oven to 160°C (310°F).
3. Place the sunflower seeds on a baking tray and bake for 8-10 minutes.
4. Transfer the seeds to a blender and blend until smooth.
5. Heat the coconut or olive oil in a pan until liquid, then add it to the sunflower seed mixture. Stir well or blend again. Optionally, add some dried rosemary for a different flavor.
6. Serve with Sunflower Seed Crackers or other low-oxalate snacks.

Nutritional Values Per Serving (2 tbsp)

- Calories: 132 kcal
- Carbohydrates: 3.5g
- Dietary Fiber: 1.5g
- Protein: 3.6g
- Fat: 12.2g

★ Grab 'n Go Snacks

Enjoy these delicious Grab 'n Go snacks, perfect for taking with you when you're out and about.

Serves 2 snacks

Ingredients:

2 pears, sliced
1 tbsp sunflower seeds
1 tbsp coconut flakes
1 tsp hemp oil
1 tbsp hemp seeds
¼ cup raisins
½ cup dried cherries

Instructions:

1. Preheat the oven to 160°C (310°F) and prepare a baking tray. Spread a bit of hemp oil on the tray.
2. Place the pear slices on the tray and bake until ready, turning them occasionally to prevent sticking.
3. Once everything has cooled, combine all ingredients in a bowl and toss well. Feel free to add other low-oxalate items to your liking.
4. Pack in a tupperware and enjoy your low-oxalate snacks when you're hungry.

Nutritional Values Per Serving

- Calories: 363 kcal
- Carbohydrates: 54g
- Dietary Fiber: 11.4g
- Protein: 5g
- Fat: 15.5g

★ Pumpkin Soup

This delicious pumpkin soup is low in oxalates and can be customized according to your preferences regarding pumpkin seeds.

Serves 2 large bowls

Ingredients:

1 tbsp. olive oil
4 cups pumpkin, peeled and diced
1 tbsp. garlic cloves
1 onion, diced
1 cup cauliflower, diced
1 cup iceberg lettuce
1 cup papaya, diced
½ cup milk
3 cups vegetable stock
1 tsp. rosemary
1 tsp. white pepper
1 tsp. Thyme

Instructions:

1. Sauté the onions in a large saucepan for 5 minutes and stir in the herbs and spices.
2. Add the pumpkin pieces and papaya, and cook for 12 minutes. The papaya adds a unique and delightful flavor to the dish.
3. Stir in the vegetable stock and milk (coconut milk can be used as an alternative). Bring to a boil and let it simmer for another 12 minutes.
4. Transfer the pumpkin soup mixture into a blender and process until smooth. Optionally, add pumpkin seeds as a topping for your Pumpkin Soup.

Nutritional Values Per Serving

Calories: 246 kcal
Carbohydrates: 36.6g
Dietary Fiber: 5.6g
Protein: 6.6g
Fat: 9.6g

★ Fruit and Fibre Soup

Experience a delightful low-oxalate soup that combines the unique flavors of cabbage and melon, creating an unusual combination that is delicious. Who knew?

Serves 2

Ingredients:

2 shallots, chopped
1 garlic clove, crushed
2 cups diced sweet Cantaloupe melon or similar
2 cups chopped red cabbage
2 cups vegetable broth
1 tsp Italian seasoning or Herbs De Provence
Himalayan salt, to taste
1 tbsp. sunflower or hemp seeds

Instructions:

1. In a pot, sauté onion and garlic over low heat for 3-4 minutes until softened.
2. Add cabbage,and herbs to the pot, and cook for 4-5 minutes.
3. Pour in vegetable broth and bring to a boil, then reduce heat and simmer for 20 minutes.
4. Season with Himalayan salt.
5. Let the soup cool slightly and transfer to a blender. Blend until smooth.
6. Serve the soup warm, garnished with soaked and dried seeds.

Nutritional Values Per Serving

- Calories: 134 kcal
- Carbohydrates: 26.4g
- Dietary Fiber: 4.3g
- Protein: 4.1g
- Fat: 1.7g

★ Savory Cheese and peas

Indulge in this savory lunch mix of cheese and peas, a staple in low-oxalate diets. Easy to prepare with organic peas and seasoned with mineral-rich Himalayan salt, this delicious meal will kick-start your day.

Serves 2 plates

Ingredients:

1-1½ cups cubed cottage or feta cheese
1 cup boiled or frozen green peas
½ onion, diced
2 slices low-oxalate bread, toasted
2 tsp olive oil
1 tsp rosemary or thyme
Himalayan salt, to taste

Instructions:

1. Preheat the oven to 200°C (400°F).
2. Arrange the cheese cubes on a baking sheet, drizzle with oil, and sprinkle with herbs.
3. Bake for 15-18 minutes, then let it cool. Separately, sauté the onions lightly in butter and mix in the peas to warm them.
4. Spread butter on the toast and combine your ingredients to top it.
5. Enjoy your Savory Cheese & Peas not only for lunch but it's a funky breakfast too.

Nutritional Values Per Serving:

- Calories: 312 kcal
- Carbohydrates: 36g
- Dietary Fiber: 6g
- Protein: 19.8g
- Fat: 10g

★ Yummy Chicken Salad

Indulge in the vibrant and satisfying Yummy Chicken Salad, bursting with fresh veggies, tender chicken, and tangy flavors. A perfect combination of textures and tastes that's bound to delight your taste buds.

Ingredients:

1 cooked chicken breast, shredded
1/4 cup diced celery
1/4 cup diced red bell pepper
1/4 cup diced cucumber
2 tablespoons diced red onion
2 tablespoons chopped fresh parsley
2 tablespoons mayonnaise
1 tablespoon lemon juice
Salt and pepper to taste

What you need to do:

1. In a mixing bowl, combine the shredded chicken, diced celery, red bell pepper, cucumber, red onion, and parsley.
2. In a small bowl, whisk together the mayonnaise and lemon juice until smooth.
3. Pour the dressing over the chicken and vegetables and toss until evenly coated.
4. Season with salt and pepper to taste.
5. Serve chilled on a bed of low oxalate greens like lettuce or arugula.

Nutritional Values Per Serving:

- Calories: 380 kcal
- Carbohydrates: 19g
- Dietary Fiber: 4g
- Protein: 37g
- Fat: 18g

★ Piperade Omelet

Oh, la la! You've gotta try this amazing Piperade Omelet!

Serves 1

Ingredients:

2 eggs, well beaten
Handful sliced green and red pepper
1/4 red onion
1 large tomato chopped
Salt and black pepper
Tbsp water (secret ingredient for fluffy omelets)
Chopped basil or other herbs (optional)
Coconut oil or butter for cooking

Instructions:

1. Melt the oil or butter in an omelet pan.
2. Add onion and peppers and lightly fry for 2-3 minutes.
3. Add the tomatoes and heat through for a minute.
4. Add the water to the beaten eggs and then add egg mixture to the pan and shake it, whilst stirring.... Give it some rock n roll movement as this helps make the omelet completely fluffy.
5. When it looks set add some herbs, salt and pepper to taste and fold over.
6. Slide onto a plate, serve and enjoy.

Nutritional Values Per Serving:

- Calories: 130 kcal
- Carbohydrates: 14g
- Dietary Fiber: 3.9g
- Protein: 12g
- Fat: 14g

★ Veggie Soup with Rice

Enjoy a warm and comforting low-oxalate soup featuring white rice and a variety of tasty vegetables, all while staying within the bounds of your low-oxalate diet.

Serves 2 large bowls

Ingredients:

½ cup white rice
2 cups cauliflower florets
1 cup chopped cabbage
1 cup chopped mushrooms of choice
½ cup chopped bok choy (or lettuce if unavailable)
1 tsp. dried thyme
1 tsp. dried basil
2 cups vegetable broth
1 tsp. olive oil
3 cups water

Instructions:

1. In a large pot, heat the oil and sauté vegetables for 5 minutes.
2. Add rice and herbs to the pot, ensuring you use only white rice to maintain low oxalate levels.
3. Pour in vegetable broth, bring to a boil, and then reduce heat to simmer for about 15 minutes, stirring occasionally. Add water to adjust the consistency as desired.

4. Taste test the soup, ensuring the rice has the right texture with a slight bite.
5. Serve and enjoy your rice-enriched low-oxalate soup.

Nutritional Values Per Serving

- Calories: 288 kcal
- Carbohydrates: 47.7g
- Dietary Fiber: 11.8g
- Protein: 11.3g
- Fat: 5.4g

★ Kale Delight Soup

Embrace the goodness of kale in this low-oxalate soup that packs a flavorful punch without relying on spinach, a high-oxalate food.

Serves 2 large bowls

Ingredients:

1 tbsp. olive oil
3 cups fresh kale, chopped
1 cup lettuce or bok choy
1½ cup cauliflower florets
1 onion, chopped
1 tsp. cilantro
2 cups vegetable broth
1 cup coconut milk
Himalayan salt, to taste
1 garlic clove, minced
OPTIONAL: 1 tsp. pumpkin seeds

Instructions:

1. In a large saucepan, sauté onions, garlic, and vegetables for 5 minutes.
2. Add the remaining ingredients, bring to a boil, then reduce heat and let simmer for about 30 minutes.
3. Blend the soup until smooth.
4. Serve warm, garnishing with optional pumpkin seeds or other leaves.

Nutritional Values Per Serving

- Calories: 259 kcal
- Carbohydrates: 16.2g
- Dietary Fiber: 5.2g
- Protein: 5g
- Fat: 19.5g

★ Refreshing Lettuce and Pea Soup

Savor this light and delightful soup that will leave your taste buds satisfied.

Ingredients:

2/3 cups fresh Iceberg or Romaine lettuce, washed and chopped
1 cup mixed vegetables (onion and butternut squash)
1 cup green peas
2 cloves garlic, minced
2 cups vegetable stock
1 cup coconut milk
Himalayan salt and (white!) pepper

Instructions:

1. In a saucepan, sauté garlic and onion for a few minutes until they begin to brown.
2. Stir in the remaining ingredients and let it simmer for about 20 minutes.
3. Using a blender or immersion blender, purée the soup until smooth.
4. Serve and enjoy immediately.

Nutritional Values Per Serving

- Calories: 105 kcal
- Carbohydrates: 13.5g
- Dietary Fiber: 3.1g
- Protein: 7.2g
- Fat: 2.2g

★ Savory Mushroom and Sage Soup

Indulge in this beautiful low-oxalate soup that is not only visually appealing but also full of delicious flavors.

Serves 2 large bowls

Ingredients:

2 cups chopped mushrooms
1 cup chopped curly kale
1 zucchini, diced
2 cups shredded red cabbage
Small bunch cilantro to taste, chopped
1 cup chopped bok choy
1 tsp. dried sage
2½ cups vegetable broth
1 tsp. olive oil
Himalayan salt, to taste
3 cups water

Instructions:

1. In a large saucepan, sauté vegetables and mushrooms in olive oil for a few minutes, then add cilantro and sage. Cook for an additional 6-10 minutes.
2. Pour in the vegetable broth and bring to a boil. Reduce heat and let it simmer for 25 minutes.
3. Add the salt.
4. Blend until smooth.

5. Serve warm, topped with a knob of butter if desired, and a side of our Crispy Crackers or your fav low oxalate bread.

Nutritional Values Per Serving

- Calories: 66 kcal
- Carbohydrates: 11g
- Dietary Fiber: 3.5g
- Protein: 5g
- Fat: 1.5g

★ Savory Slow-Cooked Beef

Indulge in this flavorful dish prepared in a slow cooker, with apple cider vinegar enhancing the taste while also ticking the low-oxalate box.

Serves 2

Ingredients:

500g beef shin (or other cut of beef if you prefer. We like beef shin as often a little cheaper and still good in the slow cooker)
Himalayan salt, to taste
1 tsp Apple Cider Vinegar
1 tsp. mustard
Drizzle olive oil
A touch of lemon juice
1 small cup water
OPTIONAL: 1 tsp. dried rosemary

Instructions:

1. Combine all ingredients, including lemon and lime juice, in the slow cooker.
2. Allow it to cook for a minimum of six hours, ensuring the meat becomes tender and flavorful.
3. Savor your delectable Savory Slow-Cooked Beef.

Nutritional Values Per Serving

- Calories: 327 kcal
- Carbohydrates: 0.1g
- Dietary Fiber: 0.1g
- Protein: 53.7g
- Fat: 12.4g

★ Succulent Pork Burger Bites

These flavorful mini burgers can be made with turkey mince, but they're absolutely divine with pork. For a healthier option, choose organic meat. You can make them bigger (like in the picture) or smaller mini-burgers. Either way, they don't last that many bites!

Serves 10 Pork Burger Bites

Ingredients:

1 lb. fresh and lean organic pork mince
⅓ cup milk
⅓ cup cilantro, finely chopped
1 ½ tsp. thyme
2 cloves garlic, crushed
⅓ cup white onion, finely chopped
1 tsp. fresh basil, finely chopped
1 tsp. dried rosemary
1 tsp. sage
Himalayan salt, to taste

Instructions:

1. Preheat your oven to 205°C (400°F).
2. Combine all ingredients in a bowl. The milk helps to bind the pork and provide moisture.
3. Shape the mixture into small, even-sized burger bites using your hands.
4. Remember that smaller bites tend to be more flavorful than larger ones.
5. Bake for 25 to 35 minutes, checking periodically as cooking times may vary depending on the size and batch of the Pork Burger Bites.
6. Enjoy immediately and store any leftovers for later.

Nutritional Values Per Serving (1 medium-sized Pork Burger Bite)

- Calories: 68kcal
- Carbohydrates: 3.1g
- Dietary Fiber: 0.4g
- Protein: 9.5g
- Fat: 2.3g

★ Baked Veg and Cheese with Maple Syrup

A delightful low-oxalate dish featuring an assortment of fresh veggies, creamy cheese, and a touch of maple syrup for a hint of sweetness.

Serves 2

Ingredients:

320g of cottage cheese
2 ½ cups pumpkin, sliced into large pieces
4 kohlrabi, cut into large wedges
1 ¼ cup cauliflower, separated into large florets
2 ½ tbsp. fresh thyme
3 rosemary sprigs
1 ½ tbsp. maple syrup
1 ½ tbsp. olive oil
Salt, to taste
2 ½ tbsp. olive oil, for drizzling after cooking

Instructions:

1. Arrange all the vegetables and cottage cheese evenly on a baking tray. Preheat the oven to 195°C (385°F) and place the cottage cheese and rosemary among the vegetables.
2. Generously drizzle olive oil over the tray bake. Pour the maple syrup over the cottage cheese.
3. Season according to your preference and bake for 30-35 minutes.

4. Once the vegetable mixture is cooked, drizzle with additional olive oil and a little more maple syrup if desired. Enjoy!

Nutritional Values Per Serving

- Calories: 525 kcal
- Carbohydrates: 37g
- Dietary Fiber: 7.5g
- Protein: 32.5g
- Fat: 37.5g

★ Cauliflower Rice Thai Style

Get ready to be wowed by this Thai-style cauliflower rice!

Serves 2.

Ingredients:

- 1 head of cauliflower
- I onion chopped
- 2 cloves garlic minced
- Healthy splash of coconut aminos (in place of fish and soy sauce)
- Handful of cooked prawns
- 2 eggs beaten
- Tsp chili (optional)
- 1/2 cup of frozen mixed veg
- Few Spring onions
- Coconut oil
- Chopped tomato
- Cucumber
- Lime wedges x 2

What you need to do:

1. Core and chop the cauliflower into small florets
2. Blitz the cauli in a food processor or use a box grater if you don't have a food processor.
3. Heat some coconut oil in a skillet or wok
4. Cook the onions and garlic gently until translucent
5. Add the frozen mixed veg and cook for a couple minutes
6. Add the 'cauliflower rice' and cook over medium heat for about 3 -5 minutes until cauli it's just softened. Nothing worse than squishy cauliflower rice!
7. Add some chopped spring onions and a few prawns to the pan.

8. Now this is what the Thais do next. Push everything in the pan to one side and scramble the eggs in the pan.
9. Then combine everything together with a splash of coconut aminos and serve with some chopped tomatoes, cucumber and a wedge of lime. อร่อย (that means delicious in Thai!)

Nutritional Values Per Serving:

- Calories:258 kcal
- Carbohydrates: 15g
- Dietary Fiber: 5.4g
- Protein: 15g
- Fat: 15g

★ Prawn and Broccoli Stir Fry

Dive into the scrumptious Prawn and Broccoli Stir Fry, where succulent prawns and crunchy veggies come together in perfect harmony. A mouthwatering medley of flavors that's as delicious as it is nourishing.

Serves 2

Ingredients:

- 500g prawns, peeled and deveined
- 1 head of broccoli, chopped into bite-sized pieces
- 1 red bell pepper, sliced
- 2 cloves of garlic, minced
- 2 tablespoons of olive oil
- 2 tablespoons of coconut aminos
- 1 tablespoon of rice vinegar
- Salt and pepper, to taste
- 1/4 cup of chopped coriander

Instructions:

1. Heat a large skillet over medium-high heat. Add 1 tablespoon of olive oil to the pan.
2. Add the prawns to the pan and cook until pink and opaque, about 2-3 minutes per side. Remove the prawns from the pan and set aside.

3. Add another tablespoon of olive oil to the pan. Add the broccoli and bell pepper to the pan and sauté for 5-6 minutes, until the vegetables are tender.
4. Add the minced garlic to the pan and sauté for an additional minute.
5. Add the cooked prawns back into the pan with the vegetables.
6. In a small bowl, whisk together the coconut aminos and rice vinegar. Pour the mixture over the prawns and vegetables.
7. Season with salt and pepper to taste.
8. Cook for an additional 1-2 minutes, until the sauce has thickened slightly.
9. Sprinkle with chopped cilantro before serving.

Nutritional Values Per Serving:

- Calories:185 kcal
- Carbohydrates: 9g
- Dietary Fiber: 1g
- Protein: 2g
- Fat: 14g

★ Baked Lemon Dill Salmon

Delight in the Baked Lemon Dill Salmon, a harmonious blend of tender salmon with zesty lemon and aromatic dill, creating a truly satisfying low oxalate dish.

Serves 4

Ingredients:

4 salmon filets
1/4 cup freshly squeezed lemon juice
1/4 cup olive oil
2 cloves garlic, minced
1 tbsp dried dill
Salt and pepper to taste

Instructions:

1. Preheat the oven to 375°F (190°C).
2. In a small bowl, whisk together the lemon juice, olive oil, minced garlic, dried dill, salt, and pepper.
3. Place the salmon filets in a baking dish and pour the lemon dill marinade over the top, coating each filet.
4. Bake the salmon for 12-15 minutes, until cooked through and flaky.
5. Serve with a low-oxalate grain like white rice and steamed low-oxalate vegetables like green peas or cabbage.

Nutritional Values Per Serving:

- Calories: 194 kcal
- Carbohydrates: 3g
- Dietary Fiber: 1g
- Protein: 23g
- Fat:10g

★ Kohlrabi and Tofu Stir Fry

A veggie favorite of ours.

Ingredients:

2 kohlrabi bulbs, peeled and sliced into thin strips
500g firm tofu cubed
1 red bell pepper, sliced
1 green bell pepper, sliced
1 onion, sliced
2 cloves garlic, minced
1 tbsp ginger, minced
1 tbsp olive oil
Salt and pepper to taste

Instructions:

1. In a large skillet, heat the olive oil over medium-high heat.
2. Add the garlic and ginger and cook until fragrant, about 1 minute.
3. Add the kohlrabi, bell peppers, and onion and cook until tender, about 5-7 minutes.
4. Season with salt and pepper to taste.
5. Serve over a bed of low-oxalate grains like rice or quinoa. Note: If you prefer a different protein, feel free to substitute tofu with something else.

Nutritional Values Per Serving:

- Calories: 246 kcal
- Carbohydrates: 23g
- Dietary Fiber: 7g
- Protein: 20g
- Fat: 10g

★ Flippin' Lovely Coconut Pancakes

Oh my goodness, check out these Flippin' Lovely Coconut Pancakes. They're so tasty and delightful, you'll be craving them all the time.

Serves 4

Ingredients:

4 eggs
1 tablespoon coconut milk or water
Teaspoon honey or your preferred sweetener
1/4 teaspoon baking soda (optional)
1/4 cup coconut flour
Coconut oil for cooking pancakes

Instructions:

1. Chuck everything (except the oil for cooking) in your blender or use a bowl and an immersion stick blender.
2. A good tip is to always add the wet ingredients before the dry.
3. Let the wizzed mixture stand a minute or two and add more liquid if too thick. Coconut flour absorbs a lot of liquid.
4. Heat a little coconut oil in your pancake pan and pour just enough batter to cover the bottom of the pan.
5. Cook until you see bubbles and then have fun flipping them or use a spatula to turn and cook the other side.
6. Makes about 6 or 8 pancakes depending on how big your pan is (and how many land on the floor when flipping)
7. Enjoy with low oxalate fruits, yogurt or any other toppings you like. We love them with peaches.

Nutritional Values Per Serving:

- Calories: 180 kcal
- Carbohydrates: 8g
- Dietary Fiber: 16g
- Protein: 2g
- Fat: 16g

★ Quick Strawberries and Cream Delight

One of the real pleasures of this diet is that it forces you to go back to basics and savor simple ingredients and foods. Strawberries are a great addition to your low-oxalate repertoire when you're short on time, and a good portable snack. One more disclaimer: we know this is simple, and that's the point, we're trying to make this as accessible as possible for you to make the transition to low-oxalate living.

Serves 1 medium bowl

Ingredients:

½ cup oat cream
½ tbsp. honey
¼ cup coconut water
A pinch of Himalayan salt
1 cup strawberries

Instructions:

1. Blend the oat cream, coconut water, honey, and a small pinch of Himalayan salt until well mixed.
2. Pour the mixture into a bowl and top with strawberries.

Nutritional Values Per Serving

- Calories: 343 kcal
- Carbohydrates: 32g
- Dietary Fiber: 1g
- Protein: 5.3g
- Fat: 23.1g

★ Simple Oat Bars

Embrace the simplicity and delight of these low-oxalate oat bars. They may be slightly flatter due to the absence of baking powder, but that's all part of the charm. Enjoy this scrumptious treat while keeping oxalate intake in check.

8 to 12 servings.

Ingredients:

1 cup oat flour
1 cup coconut flour
½ cup coconut sugar
1/3 cup maple syrup
½ cup unsweetened apple sauce
A small amount of butter
A handful of raisins

Instructions:

1. Preheat your oven to 325°F (170°C).
2. In a large mixing bowl, combine all ingredients.
3. Melt the butter and stir it into the mixture.
4. Transfer the mixture onto a baking tray, forming a layer of even thickness.
5. Bake for 25-30 minutes, but keep an eye on it as the baking time may vary depending on the flour used.
6. Remove from the oven and let it cool for at least 20 minutes.
7. Slice and enjoy your delicious Simple Oat Bars.

Nutritional Values Per Serving (per slice):

- Calories: 213 kcal
- Carbohydrates: 18g
- Dietary Fiber: 1.2g
- Protein: 2.3g
- Fat: 12.8g

★ Refreshing Lemon and Watermelon "Ice Cream"

This is a great easy blender recipe. We call it "ice cream", but whisper it quietly, it's not really even though it has a similar consistency It's best served immediately or after a short time in the freezer. While lemon peels are high in oxalate, lemon juice is low-oxalate, making it an acceptable ingredient.

Serves 2 small servings.

Ingredients:

1 cup watermelon,chopped
1 tbsp. honey
Juice of one lemon slice (more to taste)
1 cup milk or coconut milk

Instructions:

1. Combine all ingredients in a blender, such as a NutriBullet.
2. Blend until smooth.
3. Serve immediately or freeze in a silicone container for a slightly firmer texture - but avoid freezing overnight as it will go very hard.

Nutritional Values Per Serving:

- Calories: 132 kcal
- Carbohydrates: 20.4g
- Dietary Fiber: 0.6g
- Protein: 4.3g
- Fat: 4.1g

13. FINAL WORDS: BUILDING A SUSTAINABLE LOW-OXALATE LIFESTYLE BEYOND THE 30-DAY LOW-OXALATE RESET

Congratulations on completing the *Low-Oxalate Reset* and taking steps towards a low-oxalate lifestyle! Now that you've established a routine and become more familiar with low-oxalate ingredients and cooking techniques, it's important to think about how you can maintain this lifestyle in the long term. Here are some tips to help you build a sustainable low-oxalate lifestyle:

1. Keep a food journal: Your future self will thank you. Even after the meal plan is over, it can be helpful to continue keeping track of what you eat and how you feel. This can help you identify any foods that may be triggering symptoms and make adjustments as needed.
2. Meal planning and preparation: Continue to plan and prepare meals in advance to help avoid the temptation of high-oxalate convenience foods. Consider meal prepping for the week ahead or batch cooking on the weekends to make weeknight dinners easier.
3. Keep learning: Keep educating yourself about low-oxalate nutrition and new recipes. Join low-oxalate groups and

forums, read books and articles, and watch videos to stay informed and motivated.

4. Celebrate successes: Celebrate your successes along the way, no matter how small. Maybe you tried a new low-oxalate recipe or successfully navigated a social event. Recognize and reward yourself for the positive changes you're making in your life.
5. Be gentle with yourself: Remember that changing habits and routines takes time and effort. Don't beat yourself up if you slip up or have a high-oxalate meal. Use it as an opportunity to learn and adjust your approach moving forward.

By implementing these tips, you can create a sustainable low-oxalate lifestyle that works for you.

For your next steps, why not investigate any other food intolerances you may be suffering from with our comprehensive guide.

Find Your Food Triggers: Investigate Every Food With Detailed A-Z Guide - Go Low Lectin, Low Histamine, Low Oxalate, Low Salicylate, Follow the DASH Diet, Diverticulitis Diet and More

Remember, this journey is unique to each individual, so take the time to find what works best for you and your needs. Stay positive, stay motivated, and keep up the good work.

Made in the USA
Monee, IL
07 November 2023

45944538R00077